Date: 05/22/12

SP J 394.264 BRO
Brode, Robyn.
November /

October/Octubre

By/Por Robyn Brode

Reading Consultant/Consultora de lectura: Linda Cornwell,
Literacy Connections Consulting/consultora de lectoescritura

WEEKLY READER®
PUBLISHING

Please visit our web site at **www.garethstevens.com**.
For a free catalog describing our list of high-quality books, call 1-800-542-2595 (USA) or 1-800-387-3178 (Canada). Our fax: 1-877-542-2596

Library of Congress Cataloging-in-Publication Data
Brode, Robyn.
    [October. Spanish & English]
    October / by Robyn Brode ; reading consultant, Linda Cornwell — Octubre / por Robyn Brode ; consultora de lectura, Linda Cornwell.
       p. cm. — (Months of the year — Meses del año)
    English and Spanish in parallel text.
    Includes bibliographical references and index.
    ISBN-10: 1-4339-1938-9   ISBN-13: 978-1-4339-1938-1 (lib. bdg.)
    ISBN-10: 1-4339-2115-4   ISBN-13: 978-1-4339-2115-5 (softcover)
    1. October—Juvenile literature.   2. Holidays—United States—Juvenile literature.
  3. Autumn—United States—Juvenile literature.   I. Cornwell, Linda. II. Title. III. Title: Octubre.
GT4803.B7695   2010b
394.264—dc22   2009013989

This edition first published in 2010 by
Weekly Reader® Books
An Imprint of Gareth Stevens Publishing
1 Reader's Digest Road
Pleasantville, NY 10570-7000 USA

Copyright © 2010 by Gareth Stevens, Inc.

Executive Managing Editor: Lisa M. Herrington
Senior Editors: Barbara Bakowski, Jennifer Magid-Schiller
Designer: Jennifer Ryder-Talbot
Translators: Tatiana Acosta and Guillermo Gutiérrez

Photo Credits: Cover, back cover, p. 11 © Andersen Ross/Getty Images; title, pp. 7, 19, 21 © Ariel Skelley/Weekly Reader; p. 9 © Gorilla/Shutterstock; p. 13 © Elias H. Debbas II/Shutterstock; p. 15 © Jo DeLuca/Weekly Reader; p. 17 © Monkey Business Images/Shutterstock

Printed in the United States of America

1 2 3 4 5 6 7 8 9 10 11 10 09

Table of Contents/Contenido

Welcome to October!/
¡Bienvenidos a octubre!. 4

Fall Weather/Tiempo de otoño. 6

Special Days/Días especiales. 12

Glossary/Glosario 22

For More Information/
Más información 23

Index/Índice. 24

Boldface words appear in the glossary.

Las palabras en **negrita** aparecen en el glosario.

Welcome to October!

October is the 10th month of the year. It has 31 days. October is a **fall** month.

- - - - - - - - -

¡Bienvenidos a octubre!

Octubre es el décimo mes del año. Tiene 31 días. Octubre es uno de los meses del **otoño**.

Months of the Year/Meses del año

Month/Mes	Number of Days/ Días en el mes
1 January/Enero	31
2 February/Febrero	28 or 29*/28 ó 29*
3 March/Marzo	31
4 April/Abril	30
5 May/Mayo	31
6 June/Junio	30
7 July/Julio	31
8 August/Agosto	31
9 September/Septiembre	30
10 October/Octubre	**31**
11 November/Noviembre	30
12 December/Diciembre	31

*February has an extra day every fourth year./Febrero tiene un día extra cada cuatro años.

Fall Weather

In some places, leaves fall from trees in October. When many leaves have fallen on the ground, people rake them up.

— — — — — — — — —

Tiempo de otoño

En algunos lugares, los árboles pierden las hojas en octubre. Cuando se acumulan en el suelo muchas hojas, la gente las recoge con un rastrillo.

leaves/hojas

7

The weather turns cool in some places in fall. Kids enjoy riding bikes in the crisp air. Always wear a bike **helmet**.

— — — — — — — — —

En algunos lugares, el tiempo refresca en el otoño. A los niños les gusta montar en bicicleta en el aire fresquito. Para ir en bicicleta, siempre debes ponerte un **casco**.

 What do you like to do for fun in October?

¿Qué te gusta hacer en octubre para divertirte?

helmet/casco

In October, pumpkins are ready for picking.
Some kids go to a pumpkin patch.

— — — — — — — — — —

En octubre, las calabazas están en su punto.
Algunos niños van a recoger calabazas a
un huerto.

pumpkin/
calabaza

Special Days

People celebrate Columbus Day on the second Monday in October. This holiday honors the explorer Christopher Columbus. He sailed to new lands long ago.

- - - - - - - - -

Días especiales

El segundo lunes de octubre se celebra *Columbus Day* (Día de la Raza). Ésta es una fiesta en honor del explorador Cristóbal Colón, que navegó hasta tierras desconocidas hace muchísimos años.

Christopher Columbus/
Cristóbal Colón

In some years, **Diwali** starts in October. This Hindu festival of lights lasts five days. People light oil lamps in their homes.

--- --- --- --- --- --- --- --- --- ---

Algunos años, *Diwali* comienza en octubre. Este festival de las luces hindú dura cinco días. La gente enciende lámparas de aceite en su casa.

October 31 is **Halloween**. Halloween is a day to dress up in costumes and "trick-or-treat."

— — — — — — — — —

El 31 de octubre es *Halloween*. Es un día para disfrazarse y pedir *"trick-or-treat"* (truco o golosina).

What is your favorite Halloween costume?

— — — — — — —

¿Cuál es tu disfraz favorito para *Halloween*?

Many kids like to make **jack-o'-lanterns**.
They carve funny faces on pumpkins.

— — — — — — — — — —

A muchos niños les gusta hacer
lámparas de calabaza. Tallan caras
graciosas en las calabazas.

jack-o'-lantern/
lámpara de calabaza

19

When October ends, it is time for November to begin.

– – – – – – – – – –

Cuando octubre termina, empieza noviembre.

Glossary/Glosario

Diwali: Hindu festival of lights, when people light oil lamps in their homes

fall: the season between summer and winter, when the days get shorter and the weather gets cooler. It is also called autumn.

Halloween: October 31. On this holiday, many people dress up in costumes and trick-or-treat.

helmet: a hard covering to protect the head

jack-o-lantern: a pumpkin with a carved face, usually seen on Halloween

— — — — — — — — — —

casco: recubrimiento duro para proteger la cabeza

Diwali: festival de las luces hindú, en el que la gente enciende lámparas de aceite en las casas

Halloween: 31 de octubre. Este día, muchos se disfrazan y van de casa en casa pidiendo golosinas

lámpara de calabaza: calabaza con una cara tallada que suele hacerse para *Halloween*

otoño: la estación del año entre el verano y el invierno, en la que los días se acortan y el tiempo se vuelve más fresco

For More Information/Más información

Books/Libros

Autumn/Otoño. Seasons of the Year/Las estaciones del año (series). JoAnn Early Macken (Gareth Stevens Publishing, 2006)

Pumpkin Harvest/La cosecha de calabazas. All About Fall/ Todo acerca del otoño (series). Calvin Harris (Capstone Press, 2009)

Web Sites/Páginas web

Diwali Activities/Actividades para *Diwali*

www.kiddyhouse.com/Holidays/diwali
Learn all about Diwali, the Hindu festival of lights./Conozcan todos los detalles sobre *Diwali*, el festival de las luces hindú.

Pumpkin Shape Book/Libro de la calabaza

www.enchantedlearning.com/subjects/plants/types/ pumpkin/shapebook
Make a pumpkin book with fun facts./Hagan un libro con datos curiosos sobre las calabazas.

Index/Índice

bikes 8
Columbus Day 12
Diwali 14
Halloween 16, 18

jack-o'-lantern 18
leaves 6
pumpkins 10, 18
weather 6, 8

bicicletas 8
calabazas 10, 18
Columbus Day (Día de la Raza) 12
Diwali 14

Halloween 16, 18
hojas 6
lámpara de calabaza 18
tiempo 6, 8

About the Author

Robyn Brode has been a teacher, a writer, and an editor in the book publishing field for many years. She earned a bachelor's degree in English literature from the University of California, Berkeley.

Información sobre la autora

Robyn Brode ha sido maestra, escritora y editora de libros durante muchos años. Obtuvo su licenciatura en literatura inglesa en la Universidad de California, Berkeley.